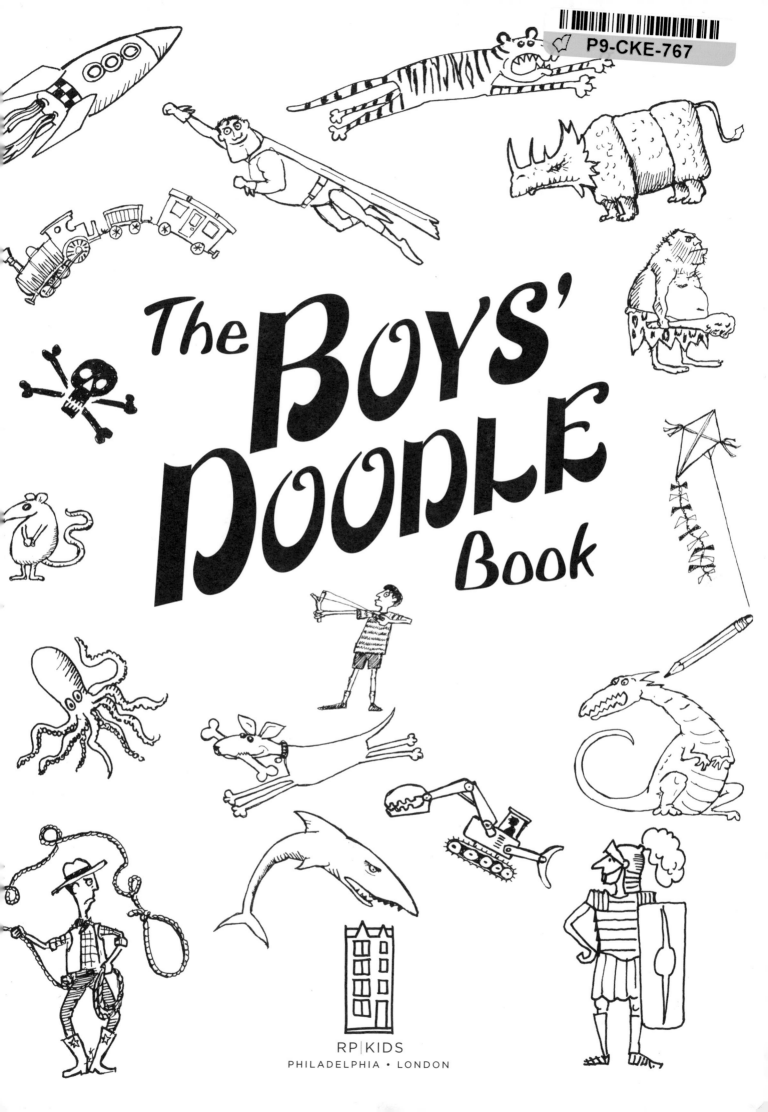

The Boys' Doodle Book

RP | KIDS
PHILADELPHIA • LONDON

15   14   13   12   11   10
Digit on the right indicates the number of this printing

ISBN 978-0-7624-3506-7

Illustrated by Andrew Pinder

This edition published by Running Press Kids,
an imprint of
Running Press Book Publishers
2300 Chestnut Street
Philadelphia, PA 19103-4371

Visit us on the web!
www.runningpress.com

Invent a robot.

Alien invasion!

Make their shields scary.

Add Wild Bill's bucking bronco.

Whoops!

Help! Get me out of here.

Mmmm, lunch.

Shiver m'timbers—what's in the chest?

Who is your hero?

What is nibbling his toes?

Finish the castle.

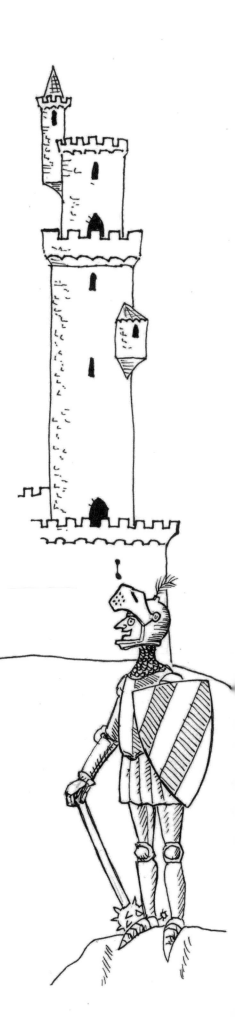

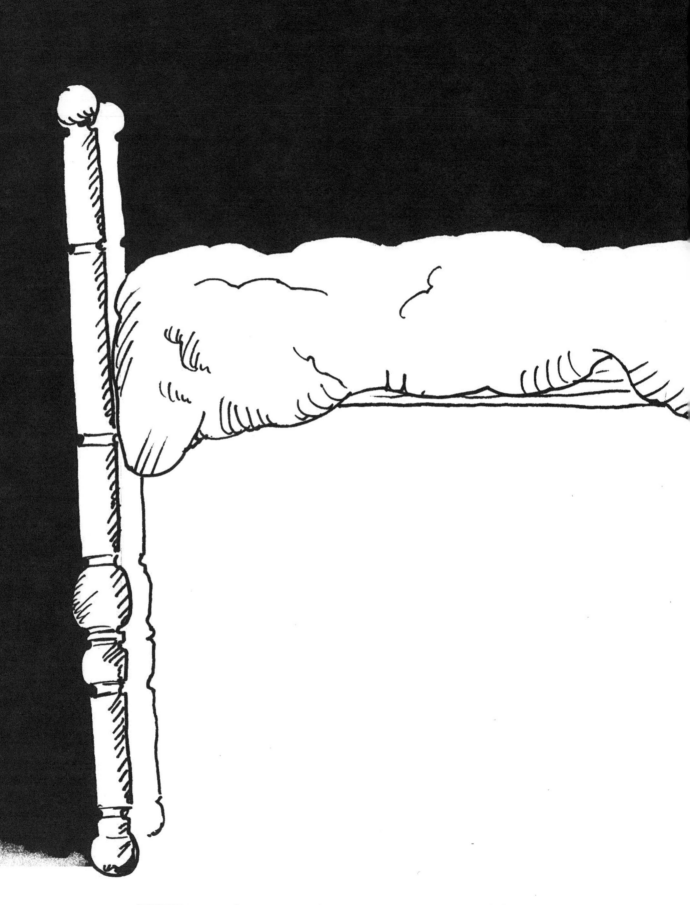

What's under the bed?

Wanted

DEAD OR ALIVE

ONE-EYED JAKE

$1000

REWARD

Draw Dr Frankenstein's monster.

At last, Herr Doctor, it lives!

EYE BALLS

What's down there?

Design their superhero costumes.

What spooked him?

What's he laughing at?

What are the lions hunting?

Retreat!

What is hunting the lions?

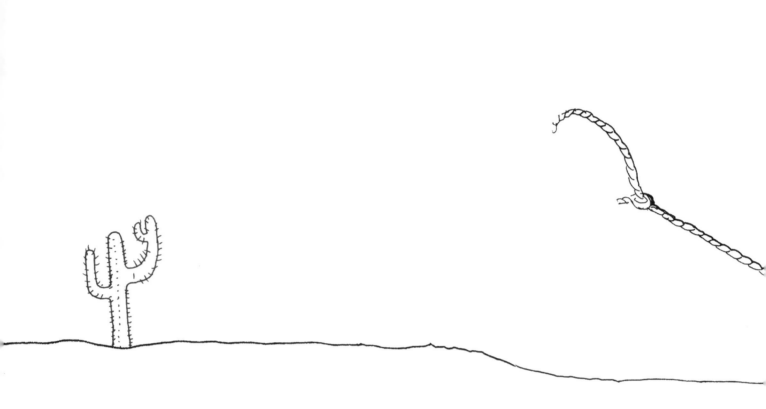

What did he lasso?

Ship ahoy!

Sketch in some slimy specimens.

Build them a space city . . .

... and their dogs a space kennel.

Yuk!

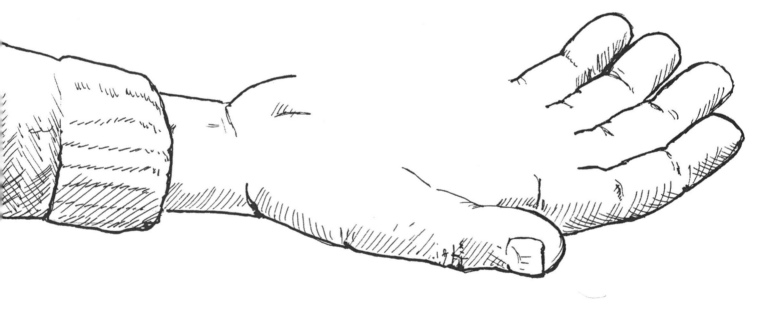

Who is hunting for presents?

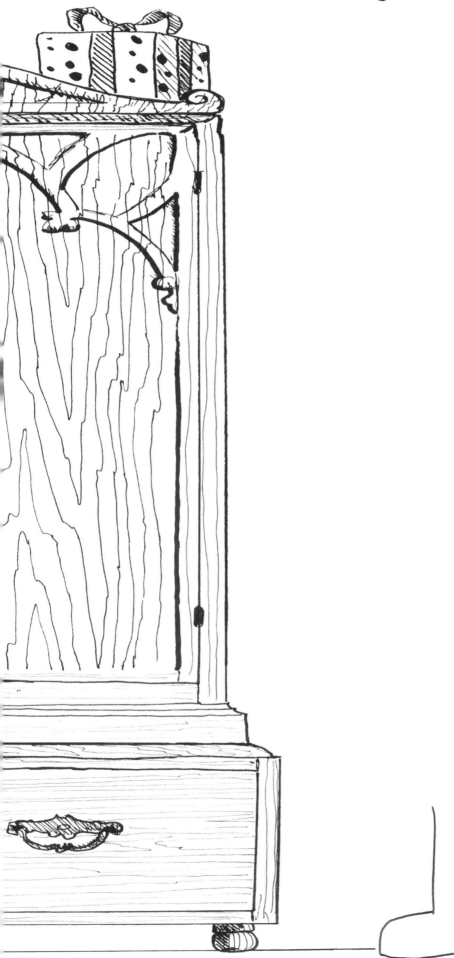

Finish the toboggan run.

What is his excuse?

He shoots . . . he scores!

Who is watching Coco the Clown?

Abracadabra!

Draw a dreadful dragon.

What did he do?

What hatched from the dino-eggs?

Draw him some armor.

Surf's up!

What's in the cave?

Finish the treasure map.

Make his hair look cool.

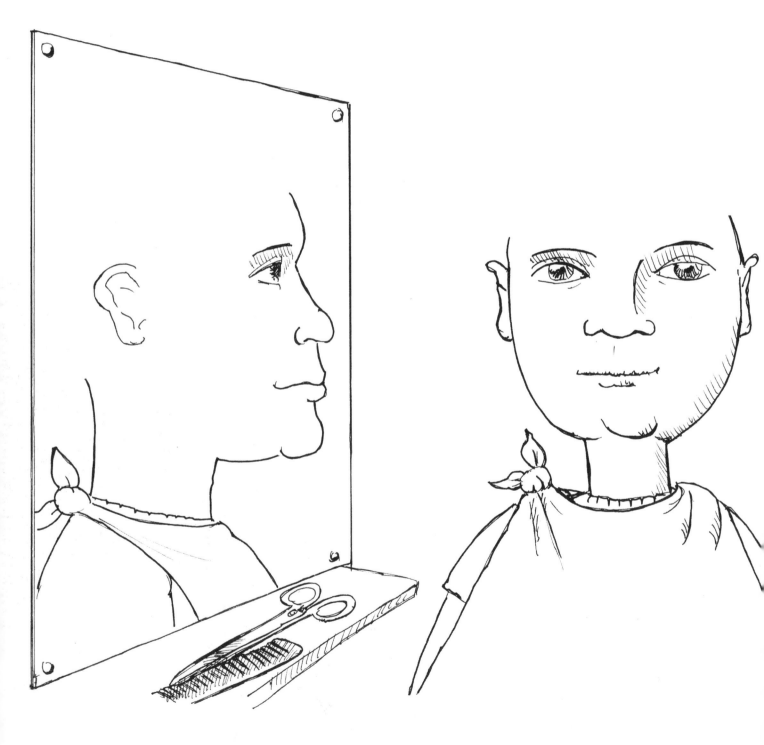

Sweet dreams . . .

Who is sitting on the eggs?

What's happening in the castle?

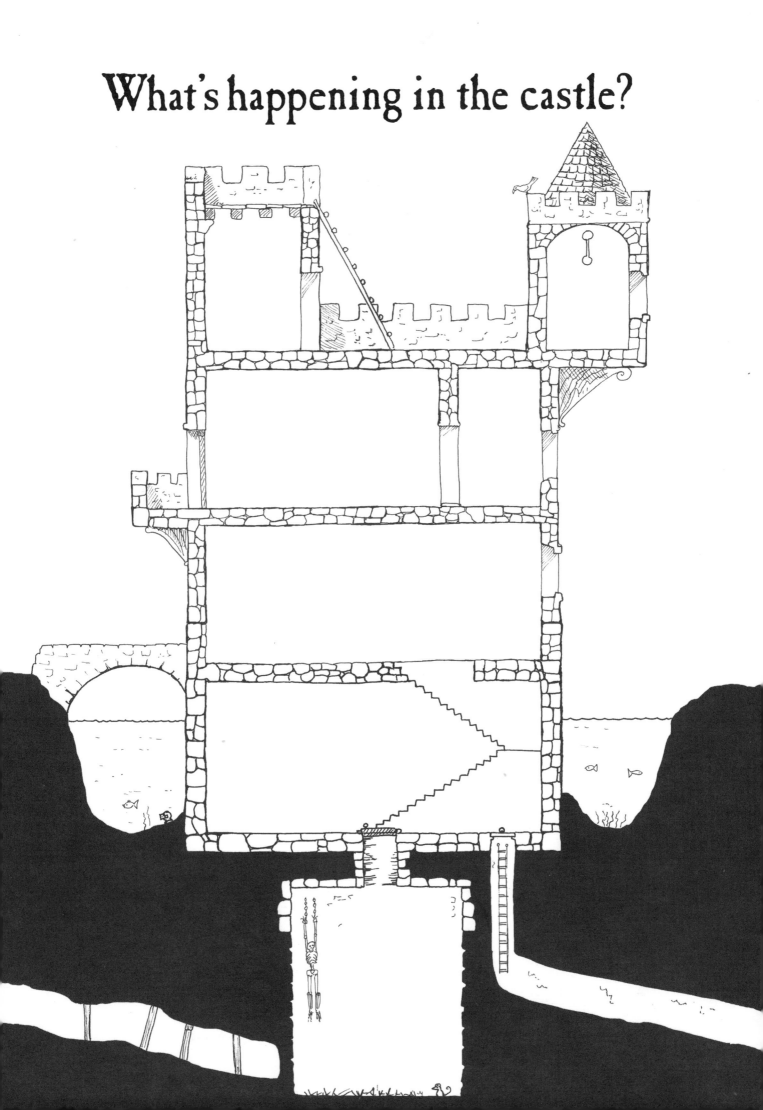

My perfect vacation . . .

Left a bit. Right a bit.

Complete the circus trick.

Launch the rocket.

Complete the monster.

What did these ants build?

Very pleas—ant.

Construct a cool tree house.

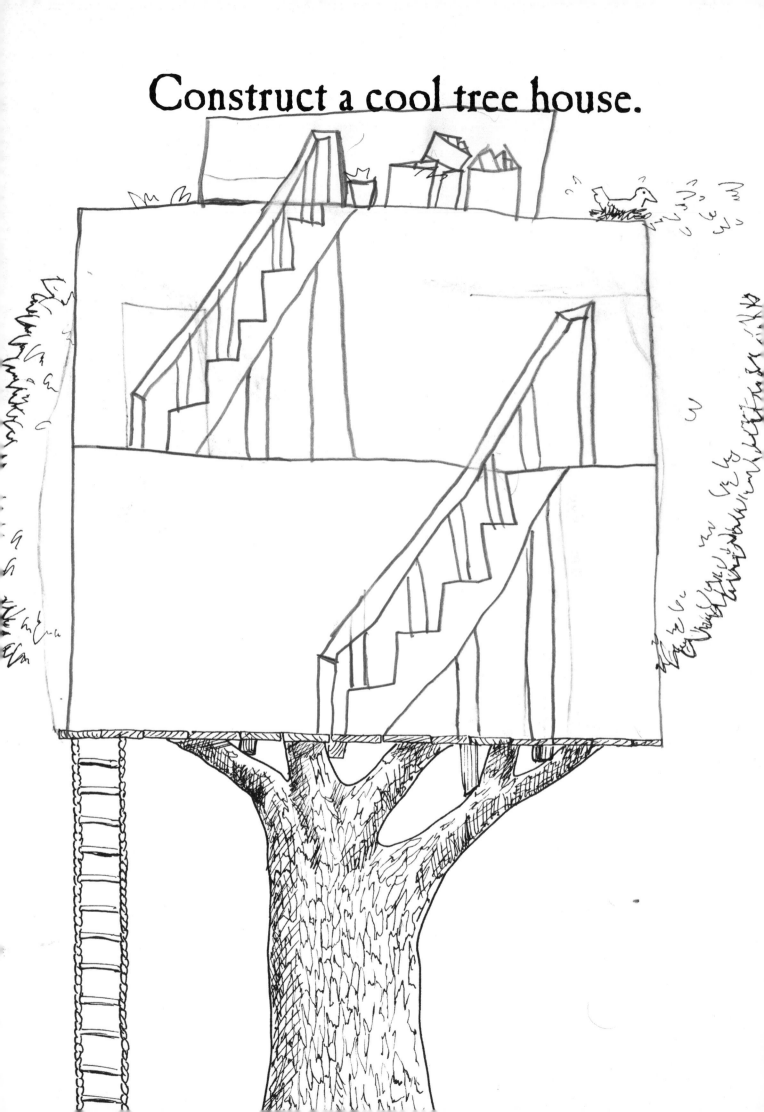

Who is visiting the haunted house?

Fix the bridge and save the people.

What is he jumping over?

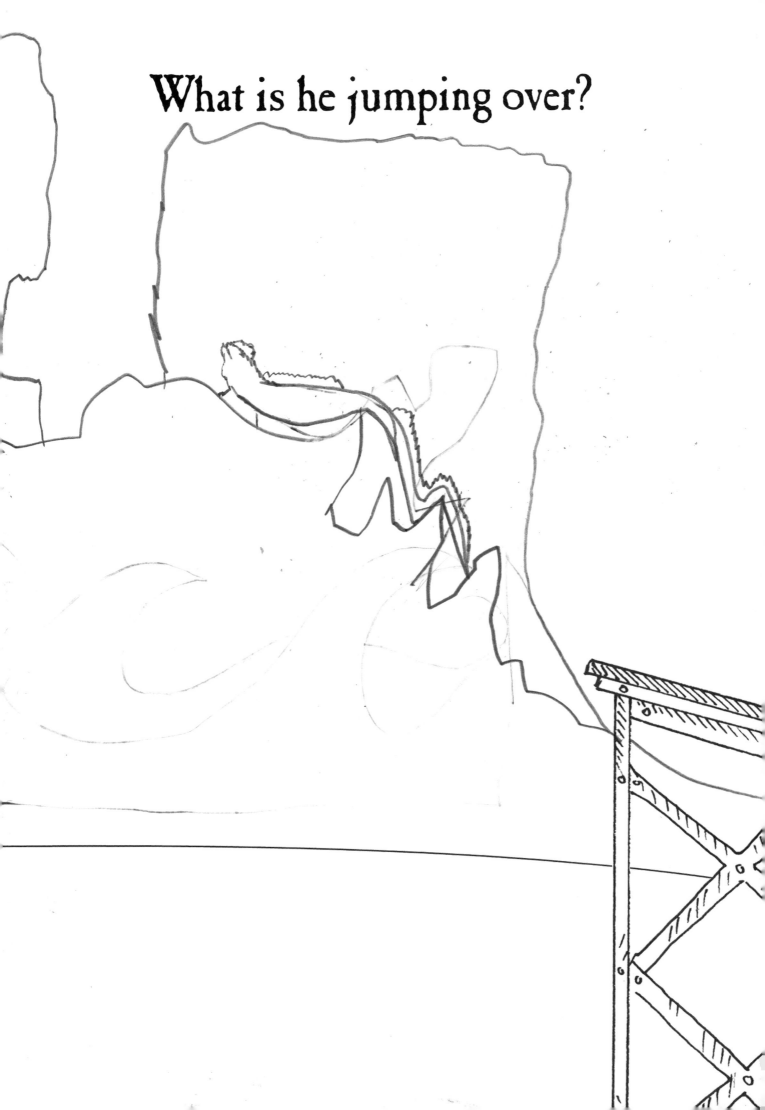

What is twisting in the tornado?

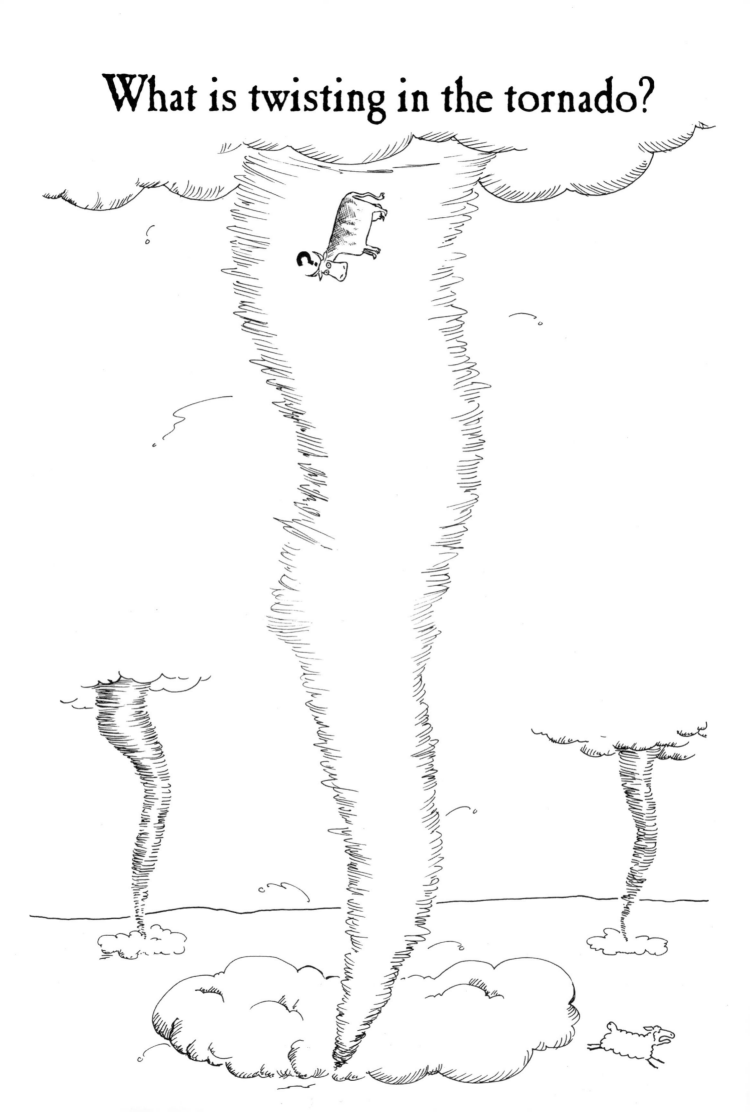

Design a great gadget.

What went bang in the night?

Draw their dinner . . .

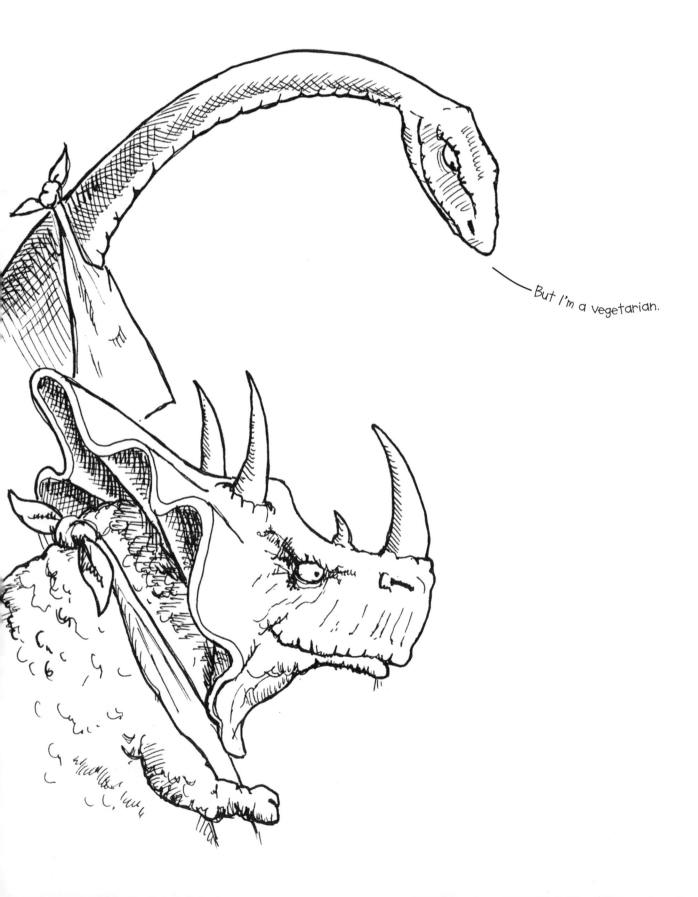

But I'm a vegetarian.

. . . and their dessert.

Just a small slice for me.

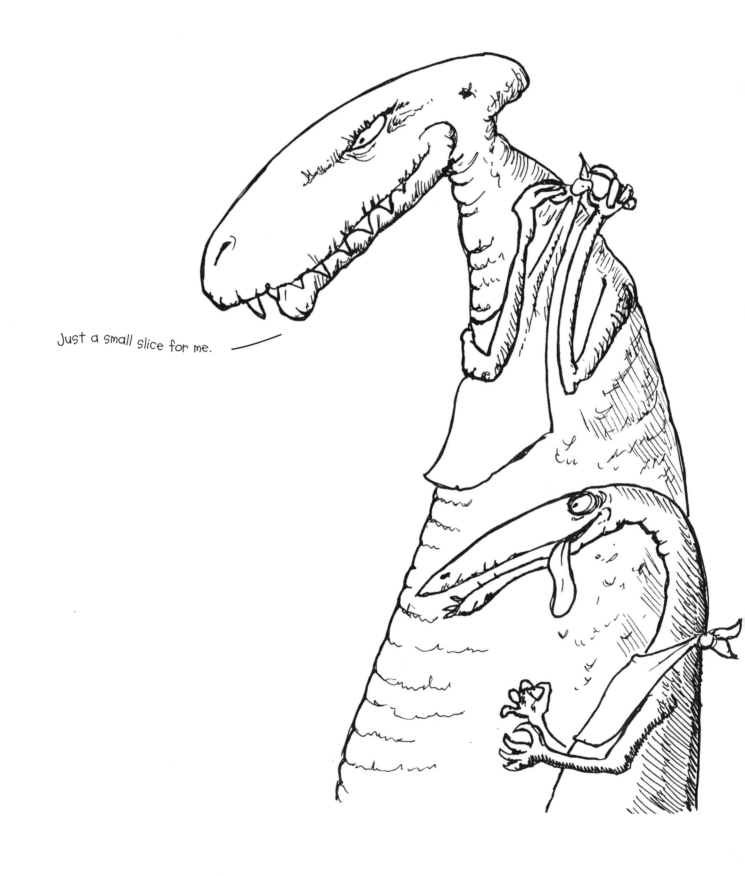

What a weird alien.

Draw his planet.

Oh no! A supervillain.

Bring a superhero to the rescue.

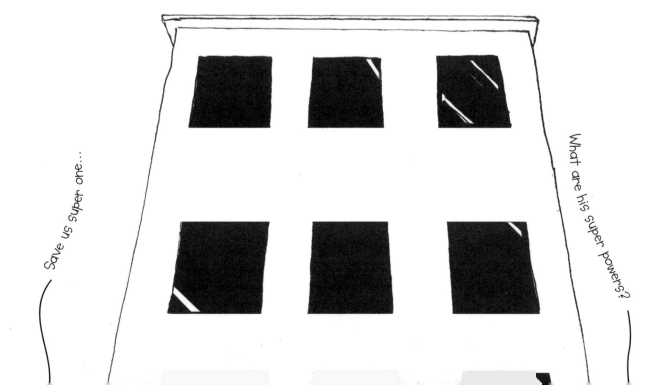

Save us super one...

What are his super powers?

Who is crossing the river . . .

What scared him?

Yikes!

Leg it!

What is he lifting?

Where are they visiting?

Design a monster truck.

Captain Jack.

No comment.

What is eating the bait?

Why is the caveman fleeing?

Finish the balls.

Complete the Viking fleet.

What's cooking?

Draw the fire brigade . . .

... putting out the fire.

Stop the thief.

What is happening in the big top?

What's in the haunted mine?

Can you stop the stampede?

Darn it.

Disguise the spy.

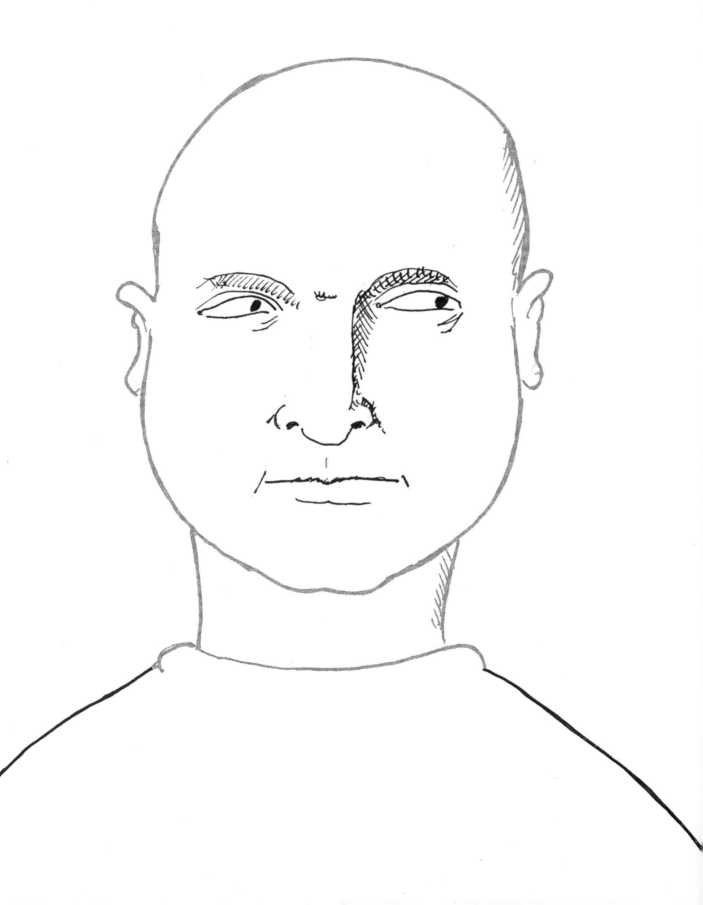

Top a brilliant pizza for yourself . . .

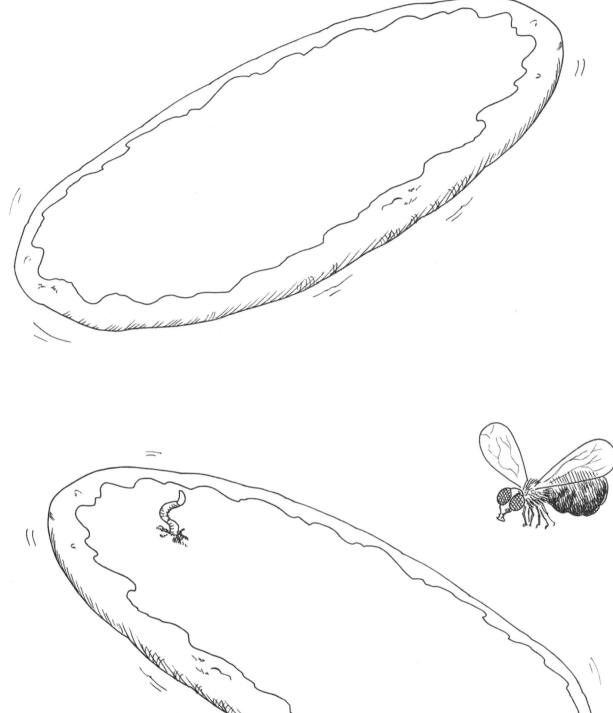

. . . and a disgusting one for someone else.

What's in the pyramid?

Design the scariest roller coaster ever.

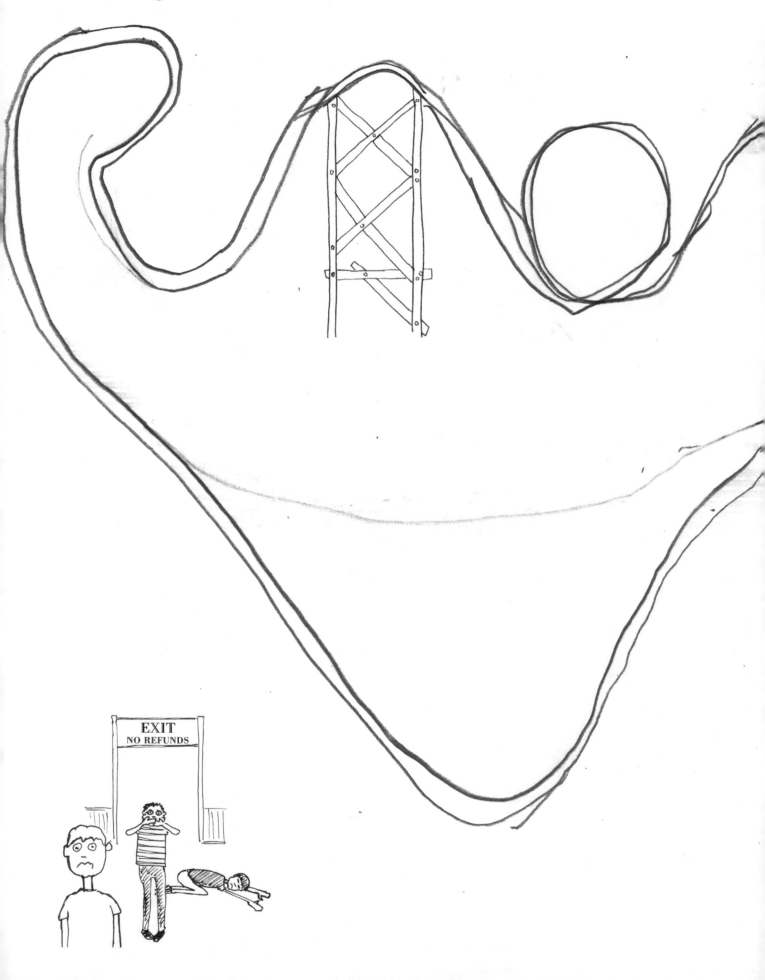

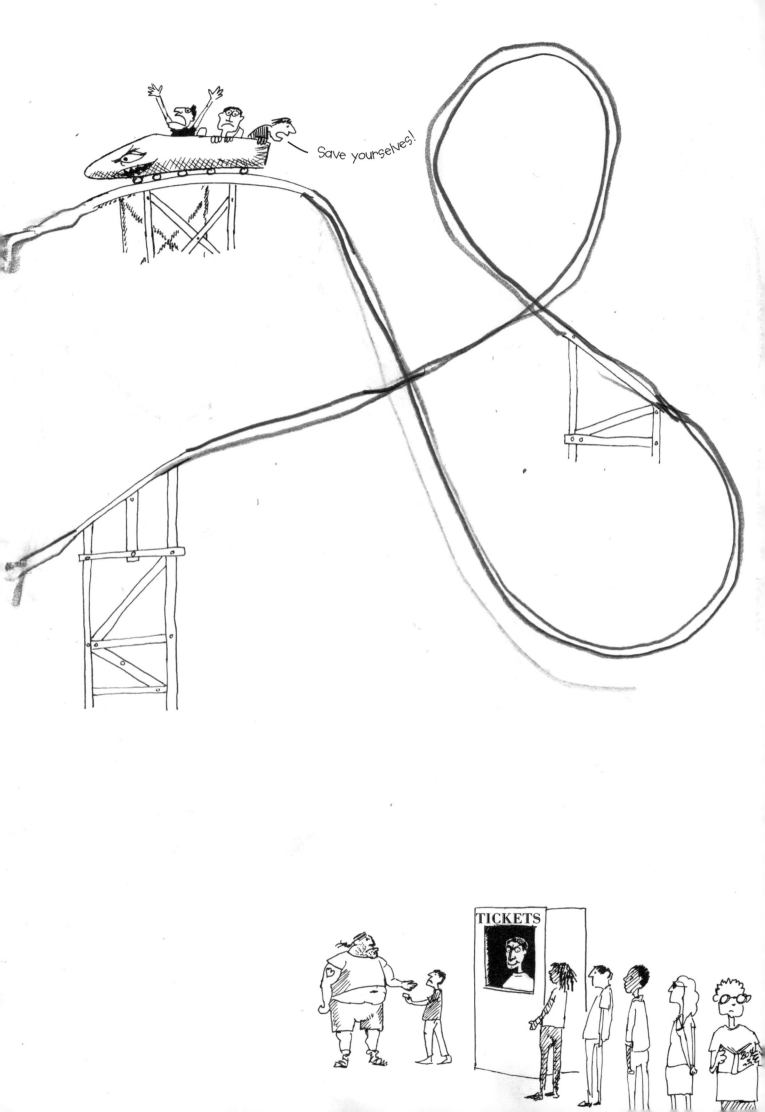

Who is bouncing?

Where are they going to land?

Not quite where I planned.

Invent a huge ice cream.

Why is he going bananas?

Who is next in the mud bath?